PIRAT
LIFE AT S

D1649873

Contents

Written by Sean Callery

Illustrated by Gabriele Antonini

Introduction

Pirates are sailors who rob other ships at sea. There have always been pirates and there are still some around the world today.

The most famous pirates sailed the seas about 300 years ago. They attacked **merchant ships** carrying gold, silver, jewels, spices and cloth.

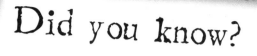

Did you know?

Most pirates were men, but a few were women. They dressed, worked and fought just like men.

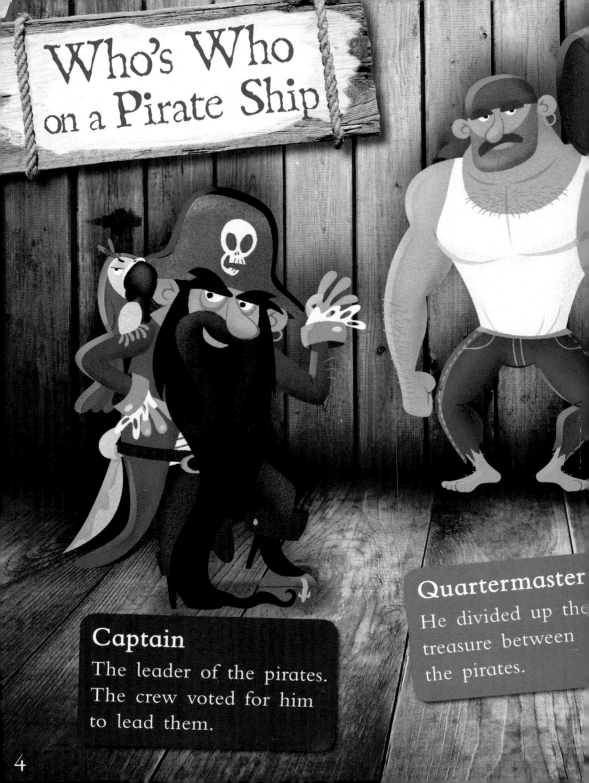

Who's Who on a Pirate Ship

Captain
The leader of the pirates. The crew voted for him to lead them.

Quartermaster
He divided up the treasure between the pirates.

4

Cook

He cooked the food. He was often a pirate who had been hurt in an attack and couldn't fight anymore.

Cooper

He made barrels for storing things like water, meat and gunpowder.

Carpenter

He mended the ship so it could sail.

Pirate Ships

flat bottom for sailing in shallow water so the pirate ship could escape from bigger ships

Many pirate ships were small and fast so they could chase and catch other ships. Some had as many as 100 pirates on board, so they could be very crowded!

crow's nest where sailors could watch out for pirates

lots of space for **cargo** in the hold

Many merchant ships were larger and slower than pirate ships and had much smaller **crews**. They did not stand a chance against a fierce pirate crew

Pirate Flags

Pirates used flags to trick the ships they attacked.

1

First, they would fly the flag of a friendly ship. They would sail up close to the other ship.

Did you know?

The pirate flag was called a Jolly Roger. The skull and bones on it were meant to scare people.

2

Then they would fly a black flag. This meant "Surrender!" Most ships would give up because they did not want to fight the pirates.

3

If the ship did not surrender, the pirates would fly a red flag. This meant "We will attack!"

Life on a Pirate Ship

Life on a ship was hard. Sailors had to climb ropes high above the deck to put up the sails and take them down again, even in a storm.

They were often cold and wet, and sometimes ill or hurt. They were always afraid of being attacked, too.

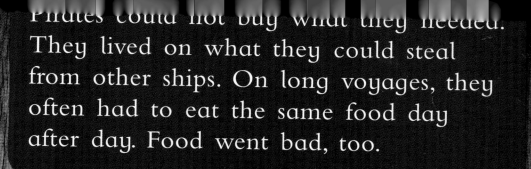

Pirates could not buy what they needed. They lived on what they could steal from other ships. On long voyages, they often had to eat the same food day after day. Food went bad, too.

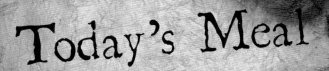

Today's Meal

Hard tack crackers
(only one year old!)

Grog
(stinky water
mixed with **rum**)

Salted meat
(going green!)

On the High Seas

It was very easy to get lost sailing across the seas, but pirates had ways of finding out where they were going.

compass to check that the ship was going the right way

map showing where there were dangerous rocks under the water

spyglass for spotting land and ships to rob

13

Pirate Rules

All pirates had to follow a set of rules.

- Keep guns and swords clean
- Share out food and water equally
- Do not fight
- Do not play cards for money
- Do not steal another pirate's treasure

Pirates did not get paid. Instead, they shared out the treasure they had stolen. The captain got the biggest share and the quartermaster divided the rest between the crew.

Did you know?

A pirate who was badly hurt got more treasure than the others. If he had lost a finger, he got 100 coins (sometimes called "pieces of eight"). If he had lost his right arm, he got 600 pieces of eight.

Pirate Punishments

If a pirate didn't follow the rules, he would be punished. If he tried to escape from the ship or stole something from another pirate, he would be marooned. This meant he would be left on an island, with only a little food and water.

Treasure

Pirates didn't only steal gold, silver and jewels. They took anything they could use themselves or sell.

Guns, food, rope and sails were all treasure to a pirate!

If pirates captured a ship that was better than the one they had, they kept it!

A Pirate Hall of Fame

These are some of the most famous pirates who ever lived.

Captain Kidd was paid to hunt pirates but he started to rob ships himself.

Ching Shih was a woman pirate. She was in charge of many ships and pirates.

Edward Teach was also known as Blackbeard. He tied bits of burning rope to his hat and beard so that he looked scary when he attacked ships.

Bart Roberts, also known as Black Bart, dressed like a gentleman but robbed over 400 ships in less than four years.

Pirate Facts: True or False?

Some of the stories about pirates are true and some are false.
Do you know which is which?

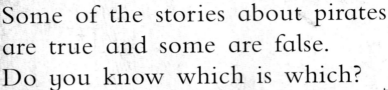

Pirates buried treasure.

Pirates kept parrots.

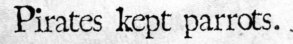

Some pirates had wooden legs.

Pirates made their victims walk the plank.

True
Pirates were often hurt in fights and sometimes had to have a leg cut off.

False
Victims were killed and thrown into the sea.

True
Parrots made good pets at sea.

False
They spent it as fast as they could.

Glossary

merchant ship
ship that carries goods to be sold

cargo
things carried on a ship

crew
all the sailors on a ship

rum
an alcoholic drink

spyglass
small hand-held telescope to help
pirates see a long way